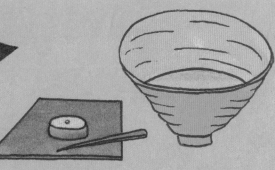

ABOUT TUTTLE
"Books to Span the East and West"

Our core mission at Tuttle Publishing is to create books which bring people together one page at a time. Tuttle was founded in 1832 in the small New England town of Rutland, Vermont (USA). Our fundamental values remain as strong today as they were then—to publish best-in-class books informing the English-speaking world about the countries and peoples of Asia. The world has become a smaller place today and Asia's economic, cultural and political influence has expanded, yet the need for meaningful dialogue and information about this diverse region has never been greater. Since 1948, Tuttle has been a leader in publishing books on the cultures, arts, cuisines, languages and literatures of Asia. Our authors and photographers have won numerous awards and Tuttle has published thousands of books on subjects ranging from martial arts to paper crafts. We welcome you to explore the wealth of information available on Asia at www.tuttlepublishing.com.

Published by Tuttle Publishing, an imprint of Periplus Editions (HK) Ltd.

www.tuttlepublishing.com

Library of Congress Cataloging-in-Publication Data for this title is in progress.

ISBN 978-4-8053-1216-2

Many thanks to Hino Nishioji Primary School, Omi Merchants Museum of Gokasho, Koga Ninja Village, calligraphy teacher Junko Funakawa, Toshiro Otowa, Goki Otowa, and Yuki Otowa. Finally, thanks to my family, neighbors, and citizens of Hino Town for your support.

Illustrations were painted with watercolor on white cotton watercolor paper.

First edition
22 21 20 19   10 9 8 7 6 5 4 3   1811EP
Printed in Hong Kong

Distributed by

North America, Latin America & Europe
Tuttle Publishing
364 Innovation Drive
North Clarendon, VT 05759-9436 U.S.A.
Tel: 1 (802) 773-8930
Fax: 1 (802) 773-6993
info@tuttlepublishing.com
www.tuttlepublishing.com

Japan
Tuttle Publishing
Yaekari Building 3rd Floor S-4-12 Osaki
Shinagawa-ku Tokyo 141 0032
Tel: (81) 3 5437-0171
Fax: (81) 3 5437-0755
sales@tuttle.co.jp
www.tuttle.co.jp

Asia Pacific
Berkeley Books Pte. Ltd.
3 Kallang Sector #04-01/02
Singapore 349278
Tel: (65) 6280-1330
Fax: (65) 6280-6290
inquiries@periplus.com.sg
www.periplus.com

Written and illustrated by Rebecca Otowa

MY AWESOME JAPAN ADVENTURE

A DIARY ABOUT THE BEST 4 MONTHS EVER!

TUTTLE Publishing

Tokyo | Rutland, Vermont | Singapore

Off to Japan!

September 1

I'm on my flight to Japan (YEAH!) and on the first page of my new notebook. For the next 4 months it will NEVER leave my side! I'm going to write down everything about my time with the Muratas. I've been emailing with Daisuke for months. He's 11 and in 5th grade like me. I really hope we'll be best buds. He lives in a small town outside Kyoto with his mom & dad & sister Mari, who's 9. My head is just about splitting from trying to imagine what Japan will be like! I have a ton of questions like:

- ☺ How much homework do they get in 5th grade? (very important to know)
- ☺ What kind of snacks do Japanese people eat? and can I get fries there? (also important)
- ☺ Do the Muratas wear Japanese clothes? (and if they do, will I have to?)

It's fun being on the plane by myself. The dinner they served had these noodles. I've never eaten cold noodles before, but there was some really hot (HOT HOT!) green mustard. It's called "wasabi". I want to write down this kind of stuff as quick as I can so my memory will be fresh

Before Dan's plane lands, here are some FACTS ABOUT JAPAN!

4 main islands	Japan is in the Pacific Ocean, off the east coast of China and Korea.
	It's about 145,000 square miles in area. You could fit 30 Japans into the USA!
	There are about 127,076,200 people. Japan is crowded!
	The people speak Japanese and some English.
	Money: the Yen (about 80–110 yen = 1 U.S. dollar)
	Sports: baseball, soccer, sumo, judo, karate
	Industry: electronics, cars, construction, service, tourism, fishing
	Religions: Shinto, Buddhism, Christianity
	Japan has many mountains and about 10% of the world's active volcanoes!

One day has already gone by, and I didn't even do anything. That's because we crossed the International Date Line, so it's already tomorrow. I'm really sleepy but I have to write something!

The whole Murata family was waiting for me at the arrival area. Mr. and Mrs. M. are really nice. They helped me change some money to Japanese yen right away. Daisuke is great! He's a little taller than me, what a surprise! Mari is kind of little for 9 and looks like her mom. The whole family spent some time in Canada for Mr. M's job, so they all speak English and, man, am I glad!

It took about 2 hours to get to their house. In Japan the steering wheel is on the right, and they drive on the left side of the road! It was night so I couldn't see much, but the buildings seem to be jumbled up and very close together. Lots of Japanese signs.

IMPRESSIONS

People remove their shoes when entering their homes to keep dirt out of the house, because many activities are done on the floor.

...soon as we got to the house, I ...to take my shoes off and put on ...pers. There are a whole bunch of ...per rules. You can't wear them on ...straw mats, and you have to ...nge slippers in the kitchen and rest-...m. I better pay attention — I don't ...nt to get these slippers mixed up!

We relaxed in the living room (big chairs!) and we kids had a glass of milk. Then it was bath time. Mrs. M. showed me how to wash myself outside the bathtub first. You don't get into the bathtub till you're clean! The water was very hot and smelled like flowers.

...ryone in the ...mily uses the ...me bath water, ...ich is why they ...e to get very ...an before the ...axing soak.

Houses are made of wood or concrete, and some doors and walls are made of paper!

Many Japanese homes have beds, but futons are often laid out for guests.
  a. Over-futon
  b. Dan in his pajamas
  c. pillow
  d. Sheet
  e. Under-futon (cotton batting)
  f. Under-futon (foam)
  g. Tatami matting on floor

a
b & c
d
e
f

I'm writing this in my futon. It's a sleeping mat on the floor, but really comfortable. Daisuke is going to sleep next to me just for tonight — it's like camping out. Tomorrow I'll be on my own! Good Night!

z
zzz

9

JAPANESE BREAKFAST

Today is Saturday, so we all had breakfast together. Mrs. M. made a big Japanese-style breakfast. The only thing I recognized was

FISH, either fresh or salted, broiled for break— Today the Mura— are having salm—

SALAD is a recent addition to the Japanese breakfast. Traditionally, they mainly eat cooked vegetables.

SEAWEED is a big part of the Japanese diet. There are many kinds. This is nori (laver) pressed into crispy, paper-thin sheets.

RICE is the st— food of Jap— Most people— it every da— Japanese ric— sticky so it— easier to pic— with chopsti—

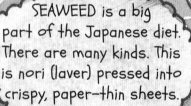

the salad (for breakfast?) but I decided to try everything. The word here is SALTY! The soup, fish, seaweed and pickles were all way salty. I was surprised because at home breakfast foods are mostly sweet. My favorite was the pickles. Mrs. M. makes them herself. The Muratas grow their own rice too. They said it'll soon be time for the rice harvest.

We ate with chopsticks. I'm glad I got some practice at the Chinese restaurant before I came! Japanese chopsticks are pointier than Chinese ones.

I'm going to take it easy today because I'm super tired. Mr. M. said I have jet lag. It's the middle of the night back home right now! He said it'll take my body a few days to get used to the change. Who'd have thought you could get this tired just from sitting in an airplane? School starts next week. Hope I'll be over the jet lag by then!

PICKLES are made of different vegetables. Flavors include salt, sugar, vinegar, miso, rice wine, red pepper, citrus, various herbs.

MISO SOUP contains miso, a salty paste made from soybeans which is dissolved in broth. The soup may contain tofu, vegetables, egg, or other things.

First week of School!!

Kids in the neighborhood meet and walk to school together. Sometimes a mom or grandpa walks along too, as a kind of safety patrol.

At the start of each class, everyone stands up and the teacher says "Now we're starting our math lesson" or whatever. Then everyone bows.

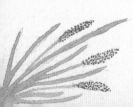

homndad@yippee.com

: japandan@yippee.com

: September 10

ve just finished my first week at Daisuke's school. It was awesome! As you can see from the
hed photos, it's WAY different from home.

y day I spend the morning in the 5th grade classroom, then after lunch and cleanup (see
)s!!!) I do my US schoolwork in another room till Daisuke comes to pick me up around 3:30.
orking out OK. Daisuke helps me out with translation in class, and some of the teachers look
me during the afternoon. A few of them can speak English, and they're teaching me some
l Japanese classroom phrases.

We eat lunch in the classroom. The food is cooked right in the school and served by the kids taking turns. The teacher eats lunch with the class!

5th and 6th grades have English
ns. They're really easy, mostly games
activities. I had to demonstrate "real
rican English"!

After lunch we have cleanup every day. At home we clean our desks, but here all the kids clean the floors and public areas, even the toilets!

ORIGAMI

You'll need: * 2 square pieces of paper, the same size. Paper MUST be square!
Small paper – small flower. Big paper – BIG FLOWER!
* glue or paste

MAKE THE FLOWER

① Make 2 diagonal marker folds. (This means fold and open again.)

② Fold all 4 corners to the center.

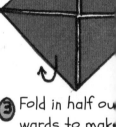

③ Fold in half outwards to make a triangle.

④ Fold in half again.

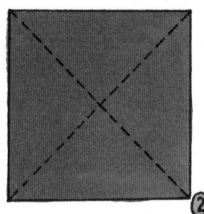

⑤ Pull on folded edge ○ so ☆ corner comes up. Flatten into a square. Do this for both sides.

⑥ Top is open, bottom is closed point.

⑦ Make small marker folds on all 4 side corners. Tuck in like a pocket.

⑧ Use a pencil to curl the 2 big points (petals) outward, and fold 2 tall points in like a pocket.

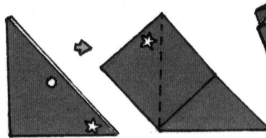

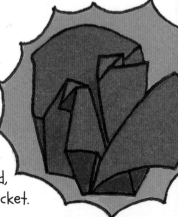

Hi! I'm Daisuke. Nice to meet you! This week in school we're getting ready for the annual Respect Aged Day party. Our class is making origami flowers for decorations. We want to make about 200 flowers. How about trying it yourself? Just follow the directions on these pages! And don't forget – the more accurately you fold, the better the result!

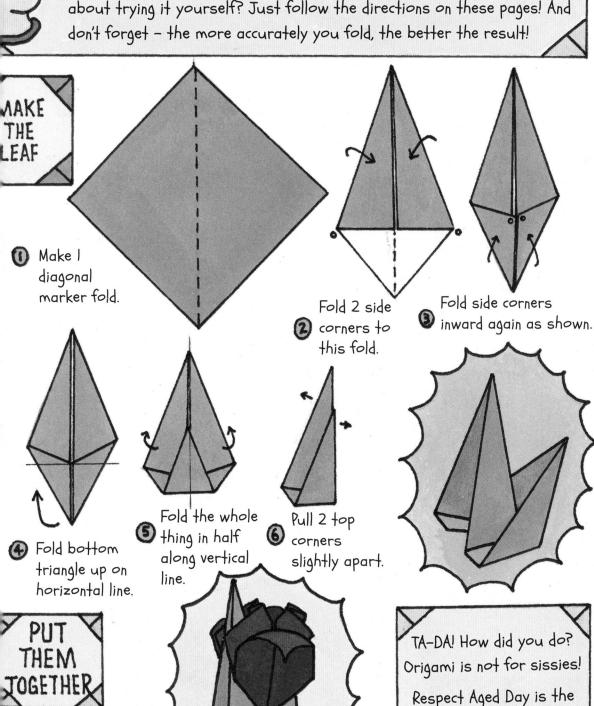

MAKE THE LEAF

① Make 1 diagonal marker fold.

② Fold 2 side corners to this fold.

③ Fold side corners inward again as shown.

④ Fold bottom triangle up on horizontal line.

⑤ Fold the whole thing in half along vertical line.

⑥ Pull 2 top corners slightly apart.

PUT THEM TOGETHER

...uck leaf tops inside ...olds of flower. Secure ...ith small drops of glue. ...ress down on flower ...ase so it stands up.

TA–DA! How did you do? Origami is not for sissies!

Respect Aged Day is the 3rd Monday of September. Give the flower to your grandmother or aunt as a present.

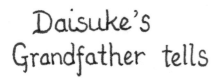

Stories

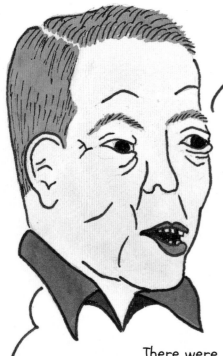

The Merchants of Omi were active in central Japan from the 1600s through the 1800s.

There were many families of merchants, and everyone in the family was involved. Boys and girls both received good educations. Boys would go on the road with their fathers from about age 15, while girls learned from their mothers how to run the big households and supervise employees and servants.

The merchants travele[d] all over Japan on foo[t] (sometimes they use[d] horses in the mounta[ins] and some even went by boat to places like Vietnam and Thailand.

They carried and sold fabrics, fab[ric] patterns, kimono[s], fans, writing pap[er], wooden bowls, mosquito nets, medicines, and te[a].

September 19

Today is Respect Aged Day and we have a day off from school. Daisuke's grandfather came to visit — he's a really together old dude — and us guys had a good time talking. Daisuke and his dad translated while Grandpa M. told me about the Merchants of Omi. They were these cool traveling merchants who came from this part of Japan long ago.

...e merchants carried
...eir wares in packs
... their backs or on
...les balanced on their
...oulders. They wore
...oad straw hats,
...ick denim capes,
...ggings, and straw
...ndals.

Most merchants were
independent, carrying
goods made in their
own districts,
although some
traveled as
representatives
of large shops.

They were very astute businessmen whose code was
known as "sanpo-yoshi", or "three-way satisfaction".
Good business was supposed to satisfy the seller
and buyer, and as well, to improve society as a whole.

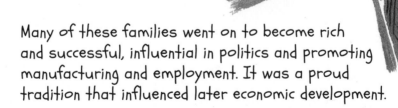

Many of these families went on to become rich
and successful, influential in politics and promoting
manufacturing and employment. It was a proud
tradition that influenced later economic development.

September 25

The past 3 days we've been working on the rice harvest. The whole family helped – Grandpa M. too. It was hard work! The rice plants were standing in water at first, but they drained the water out a few weeks ago so the fields are nice and dry. Everyone was glad about the nice weather. First, Grandpa M. "opened the field." That means cutting the rice at one corner of the field by hand so the harvesting machine can get in. I helped. We cut the bundles of stalks close to the ground using special blades.

Then Mr. M. drove the harvester into the field. It's big and red and shaped kind of like a tank. I got to ride on it with Daisuke. It's deafening! The machine cuts 3 rows at a time, collects the rice grains, and throws the cut-up straw out onto the field.

The rice is transferred to trucks with special containers mounted on them. The trucks drive to the local grain elevator for the rice to be hulled, measured, and bagged. We kept enough rice for the family and brought it home. It had to go through a dryer and then have the hulls taken off – they look kind of like dry cereal, but you can't eat them. What's left is brown rice. It's put in bags made of heavy paper and stored. Each bag weighs 66 pounds, exactly as much as me! The Muratas eat about 12 bags in a year!

RICE HARVEST

Last night Mrs. M. ran some of the rice through their home polishing machine to change it from brown to white. Then she cooked it for dinner, but before we ate, she put some in a special cup and offered it at the family shrine. Mr. M. said that's to thank the gods for the harvest. I hope they liked the rice – I sure did! The new rice is very soft and shiny. Everyone had seconds!

Some hulls and straw are collected to use in the garden. Mrs. M. and us kids did the collecting. She says they make terrific mulch. We put the bags of hulls and the bales of straw in the garage. Some people put up racks and hang the straw on them.

Grain of rice ⇒ hulled (brown) rice ⇒ polished (white) rice

Mari's Challenge

Hi! I'm Mari! Now that the rice is harvested, let's make something with it! Onigiri are balls of salted sticky rice about the size of a tennis ball. They are usually wrapped in crispy seaweed and have different fillings. Actually, "nigiri" means to squeeze, or make a fist, so you squeeze the balls into shape with your hands.

If rice is like bread to Japanese people, onigiri are like sandwiches. We take them on picnics, to the beach, on a hike, anywhere we want food that's easy to eat.

There are all kinds of traditional fillings, but you can also fill onigiri with things you can find in your grocery store. Wash your hands and let's begin!

BASIC INGREDIENT

☆ Rice – short-grain or "sushi" rice. Fo the cooking directions on the packag

☆ Seaweed – flat paperlike crispy shee called "nori" or laver. (Find these at c Asian grocery or Asian food section your local market.)

☆ Salt – any white kitchen salt is fine.

TRADITIONAL FILLIN

☆ 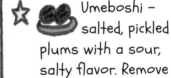 Umeboshi – salted, pickled plums with a sour, salty flavor. Remove the pits first!

☆ 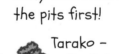 Tarako – salty fish roe. (Roe means eggs.)

☆ Katsuobus shaved drie bonito fish, mixed a little soy sauce

☆ Sake – not kind you dr This is flaked sal

Try other flavors to

☆ 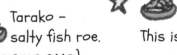 Tuna – use the kind packed in water. Squeeze out the water and mix with a little mayonnaise or mustard.

☆ Bacon bits or cr dried onion bits, both together!

☆ Finely chopped h cheese, or pas

☆ Finely chopped p (try hot ones to

Maybe you can think of other things to use as a filling! Just make sure have a strong flavor and aren't too wet.

ONIGIRI

When Dan saw this page, he said "Hey, I thought we already did this!" He mixed up the words "onigiri" and "origami". I guess they are pretty alike. LOL!

SHAPE with your HANDS

①

Spread cooked rice out in a bowl to cool slightly, and mix in salt (about 1/2 teaspoon for 3 cups of rice)

②

Japanese moms use their bare hands. They wet them first so the rice won't stick. You can also spread plastic wrap on your hand and squeeze the rice inside the wrap.

③

Use about 1/2 cup of rice. Roughly shape the ball...

④

... and then make a depression in the center.

⑤

Put in the filling, and press the ball tightly into shape. Round or triangular is traditional, but you can make oval or even cube-shaped ones!

⑥

Place a piece of nori around the ball and squeeze it so it sticks to the rice.

⑦

Wrap the finished onigiri in plastic wrap. Don't let them dry out. Eat them soon, or keep them in the refrigerator for a day or so.

October 1

Tonight was awesome! Mrs. M made a really yummy dessert and we were all just sitting around watching TV when we started talking about how we like to relax. I ended up interviewing everyone just like a news reporter! I made a chart comparing my family with the Muratas. Here it is!

WHAT DO YOU LIKE TO DO TO RELAX? in these 4 categories?

	Outdoor	Indoor	TV show	Family Outing
WILLIAMS FAMILY				car trips
Dad	tennis	Internet	sports, documentaries	
Mom	tennis (with Dad)	cooking	documentaries	
Debbie	taking care of our dogs	drawing	Animal Planet	
Me	basketball	Internet	sports	
MURATA FAMILY				hiking, going to movie
Mr. M	hiking, history walks	insect keeping	nature programs	
Mrs. M	volunteer at local tourist assoc.	crafts, cooking	movies	
Mari	bike riding with friends	drawing	anime	
Daisuke	soccer, hiking	historical manga	sports, movies	

Results of My Research!

1. Our sisters both like to draw. I'm going to set up an online exchange so they can see each other's work. I'll link up my mom and Mrs. M. so they can talk about cooking too!

2. Mr. M. actually keeps and breeds bugs. They are called "suzumushi" or "jingle bell bugs" because of the sound they make. They're a bit like crickets. He keeps them in a little bamboo cage. They're kind of noisy.

3. Daisuke loves manga about life in samurai times. He lent me one. There was a picture where a man got his arm chopped off by a sword. Cool!

4. I miss our dogs! Hey, Mitzi and Blackie! Do you miss me? Pet-wise, I'll take dogs over bugs any day!

5. I miss basketball too, but I'm getting pretty good at soccer from playing at school with Daisuke.

Relaxing with the Family

October 10

Today was a public holiday called "Athletic Day." I went with Daisuke to a kendo competition at a big sports complex. The competition took a long time, so I walked around the complex for a bit. It was completely devoted to martial arts! I got to peek in on 5 different ones. I can see why they're called "arts" and not sports. Getting the form and movements right seems to be just as important as winning. The names all ended in "do" – kendo, judo, naginatado, aikido, and kyudo – and Daisuke said that means "way", both the way to do something and a kind of spiritual practice. I didn't get that, but I noticed there was a lot of bowing. Daisuke says you have to show respect to your opponent. I don't think we're going to see that on Monday Night Football any time soon, but it was interesting.

KENDO is styliz[ed] sword fighting based [on] samurai techniques opponents try to s[core] hits on each othe[r's] body with a bam[boo]

KYUDO is stylized archery and dates from samurai times. It is the only martial art where opponents don't fight face to face. Using a long, flexible bow, players shoot arrows at a small target, competing for the greatest number of hits. The shooting area is covered but the targets are outdoors.

NAGINATAD[O] is similar to kendo, [but] the weapon is a lo[ng] pole tipped with a large curved bla[de]. In Japan, it's

. They shout when they
ck. Players wear heavy
n outfits, metal barred
ks, breastplates, and
es, but fight
foot.

JUDO is a type of wrestling that dates from the 1880s. "Ju" means "gentle". Players use throws and holds to immobilize their opponent. Strength is less important than form and strategy. The dress is a short tunic and pants.

ly a women's art. Players
r hakama (a heavy,
-length culotte). Both
o and naginatado
played indoors on
den floors.

AIKIDO was developed in the 1930s. The name means "way of unifying with life energy". Originally strictly a defensive art, it involves turning the opponent's energy back on him. Throws and holds are used. Both judo and aikido are played indoors and barefoot on special mats.

BOWING

Hi! Daisuke here! Dan's been asking me about bowing. It's really important in Japan. At my kendo lesson we bow to the teacher at the beginning to ask for the instruction, and again at the end to thank him. ("Sensei" means "teacher," but the characters actually mean "born before." I guess most teachers are older than their students!) We also bow to signal the beginning and end of a conversation, and especially when we say please and thank you. There are a lot of different ways to bow. Let's try some all-purpose ones, as well as the greetings to say when you're bowing. The key word is respect! Pretend you're paying your respects to a high-ranking samurai!

STANDING

Stand straight. Make eye contact.

Bend forward from the waist with hands at your sides. Look down.

SITTING on the floor

Sit on your folded legs and put your hands on your thighs. Make eye contact.

Slide hands down to the floor and bend forward. Look down.

TEA

Tea plants were introduced to Japan from China in the 13th century, and the tea ceremony developed in the 16th century. Tea was originally used by Zen monks to keep them awake during meditation. Later drinking tea became a social ritual of hospitality.

The tea Mari served is made from exactly the same leaves as ordinary black tea, but the processing is different. Green tea is steam-dried and then ground into a fine powder to make *matcha* used in the tea ceremony.

Here are the utensils used in the most basic tea ceremony:

A tea bowl
B tea container
C tea spoon
D tea whisk

E cold water jar
F kettle
G brazier
H water ladle

I kettle lid
J wet cloth
K lid rest
L waste water jar
M silk dry cloth

The essence of the tea ceremony is politeness. Many special words are used and the host and guest often exchange bows. Japanese people find this highly stylized ceremony both uplifting and relaxing.

Powdered green tea is mixed with hot water and whisked to a froth. It is quite bitter and is drunk without milk or sugar, so the guest eats a very sweet cake (okashi) before drinking it.

Today Mari invited me to her tea ceremony lesson. It was pretty surprising! I was a "guest" and Mari made tea for me. I sat on the tatami mat with my legs folded under me. Mari carried in lots of little pots and bowls, and sat in front of a charcoal brazier with a kettle on it. Then she wiped everything with little cloths. While she did all that I ate a very sweet cake her teacher gave me. Mari spooned this green powder into a bowl and added hot water. Then she stirred it with a bamboo thing shaped like an egg whisk. Finally she passed me the bowl. It didn't have a handle, and the teacher showed me how to hold it in both hands in a special way. There was a little bit of frothy green tea in the bowl. It was really bitter. Made me think of mom "having tea" with her friends — talk about different! Mari cleaned up the bowl and took all the things back out. There was a lot of bowing. I'm glad Daisuke taught me how to do it! But when I tried to stand up, my feet were asleep and I almost fell over! I'd been sitting there for almost half an hour! Wow!

October 29

Part I of today! We all went to a "Ninja Village" in the mountains. It was super fun, with authentic old thatched houses, a museum, and tons of great activities like a shuriken target range, wall climbing with ropes, and a pontoon water crossing. The kids at home will be green jealous when they hear how much I know about real Japanese ninja!

Ninja were not warriors but spies, information carriers, and assassins. Their specialties were concealment, quick strikes, and escapes.

A ninja escapes through a secret doorway hidden behind a decorative scroll.

Ninja use a portable rope ladder and grapples to climb a stone wall.

The homes of ninja families often had built-in secret passages, trick walls and doors, and collapsing ceilings to foil enemies or rivals. Techniques were handed down in the families and kept deadly secret.

The region Dan visited is the home of the "official" ninja families. In the 17th to 19th centuries, they were employed by the central Edo government. Other ninja groups also worked throughout Japan in this period.

the daytime, ninja
guised themselves as
mers, priests, merchants,
craftsmen and blended
local life.

grapples – for climbing walls and roofs

arrows fitted with small torches – for setting fires at a distance

brass knuckles – for hand-to-hand combat

Typical ninja tools and weapons

e well-known
ja costume
was mainly
sed at night.
was designed
camouflage,
ed, and ease
f movement.
simple black
eavy cotton
fit included a
ht hood, hand
overings, and
th socks with
thick soles.

short daggers and garroting cords – for assassinations

shuriken (meaning "the sword behind the hand") – to be thrown at pursuers

rtable pontoons
d breathing pipes –
r traveling on or
water

MICRO SUSHI

 EDOMAE or **NIGIRI SUSHI** – a bite-sized oval of sus[hi] rice with a piece of fis[h] shrimp, egg, etc. laid over the top and usu[ally] containing wasabi.

MAKI SUSHI sushi rice rolled up in a shee[t] of dried seaweed (nori) with various ingredients in the middle, then cut int[o] pieces. These can [be] very elaborate.

October 29

On the way home from the ninja place we stopped at a sushi restaurant. I've heard of "Sushi Train," but I'd never actually eaten sushi. I was pretty nervous (what if I couldn't eat the raw fish?). The restaurant was small, with a counter and a big glass case full of scary-looking things with shells, eyes and tentacles. The chef stood behind the counter making sushi to order.

MICRO SUSHI was f[irst] served to children w[ho] had never eaten su[shi] before and also tu[rned] out to be popular w[ith] Westerners. Micro s[ushi] are not very wide[ly] available, but they [are] an amazing example [of] Japanese craftsman[ship].

WHAT IS SUSHI?

Start with: rice + vinegar + salt + sugar = sushi rice

Fillings: fish   eggs vegetables   seaweed

Garnishes: horseradish   soy sauce   pickled ginger

It's quite a mouthful of interesting flavors.

SUSHI

TEMAKI SUSHI – "do-it-yourself" sushi. Rice and fillings are placed on a sheet of which is then rolled to a cone shape.

CHIRASHI SUSHI – a bowl of sushi rice mixed with fish, carrot and other tables, then topped finely sliced egg and ed ginger. Though r sushi is finger , chirashi sushi is lly eaten with sticks.

USHI

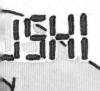

ro regular size
shi

Mr. M. said that I should try some rolled sushi to start with. He ordered small ones with cucumber and egg inside. I was surprised at how sweet it was! Then Mr. M. tried me out with nigiri-sushi topped with smoked salmon – it was kind of greasy but good. I tried some of the pickled ginger garnish too. It looks like pink flower petals, but it's very crunchy, and the taste is amazing – hot, sweet, and strong!

Meanwhile all the Muratas were really scarfing down the sushi! Daisuke's favorite is negi-toro. That's tuna meat chopped up with green onion and rolled into maki-sushi. Yep, it's raw! I was still SO not going to go there. But Mr. M. spoke to the chef and in a little while he brought me the most amazing thing! A tiny (like, matchbox size) wooden stand with five different nigiri-sushi only the size of my pinky nail. They were cool! Mr. M. said they're called "micro sushi." I ate them all – tuna, octopus, scallop, shrimp, and egg. I have to say, they were awesome! Next time I'll be brave enough to eat a regular size one.

Shodo

書道

"Shodo" means "way of writing". This same word "do" is used in martial arts. Shodo takes the same kind of concentration and discipline.

At first, Japan had no written language. Then Chinese characters were adopted around the fifth century A.D., about the same time as Buddhism was introduced. Japan still uses these characters, and also two alphabets derived from them.

There are over 10,000 characters. By the end of primary school, children already know almost 1000.

Even though the writing is very complicated, Japan has one of the highest literacy rates in the world – over 99% of people can read and write.

Japanese writing is a very important art form. There are lots of writing styles. Some are almost impossible for ordinary people to read.

Some artists use huge brushes to write very large and powerful characters.

November 5

Today was Saturday and Daisuke took me to his shodo (writing) class. It was a real quiet afternoon! All the kids were kneeling on the floor in front of big pieces of paper. They used ink and brushes to write really big characters and then signed their names. Everyone used their right hand. Daisuke said shodo is designed for right-handers. Come to think of it, that's what Mari said about the tea ceremony. Does Japan have many left-handed people??

udents begin by acticing small aracters with a pencil, study the shapes d proportions. The acher corrects sture and hand sition as well as aracter shapes.

ush work is ually done on the oor. The brush is held rtically above the per and is moved th the whole forearm. ntrol is important, it so is letting go and oving with freedom d grace.

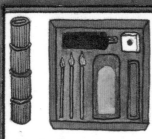

Student's writing set – brush, inkstone, water container, bottled ink, paper roll

Advanced students make their own ink using an ink block and water. This ink is very expensive and comes in many different shades of black!

Children regularly practice shodo and drawing with brushes at school.

The shodo brush can be used to draw pictures. Many of Japan's most famous works of art were done with a brush.

DAISUKE'S CHALLENGE

JAPANESE WRITING

Hi guys! I guess Dan explained about my sh[...] class. Of course we don't write that way all the time! We mostly use pens and pencils a[...] computers just like you. But Japanese writ[...] is pretty cool. We can write either up to do[...] or left to right. We also use 3 different kin[...] of writing besides regular ABCs. You can ch[...] them out here and try them for yourself.

KANJI

Kanji, or "Chinese characters", came from China, of course – more than a thousand years ago. They started out as pictures of things.

大助

DAI   SUKE

Here's my name in kanji. It means "big help" – but maybe my mom wouldn't agree!

After a while they were combined to make lots of different meanings.

田 + 力 = 男

田 (rice field) + 力 (strength) = 男 (man)
Strong in the rice field, like my dad!

宀 + 豕 = 家

宀 (roof) + 豕 (pig) = 家 (house)
Where the pigs are——! Kind of funny, huh?

女 + 子 = 好

女 (woman) + 子 (child) = 好 like or love
I guess that's about right.

EVOLUTION OF KANJI

 → 月 moon

 → 日 sun

 → 山 mountain

 → 馬 horse

NOW YOU TRY IT!

(you can copy or use tracing paper)

NI   HON

Nihon means Japan, "land of the rising sun"

NIN   JA

Ninja! (can you find the "sun" in this word?)

Japanese kids have to know about 900 kanji by sixth grade!

Hiragana

In Japanese writing, kanji tells you the meaning and [hir]agana tells you the sound. It's also used to write [wor]d endings. There are 47 hiragana letters.

[For] example, ありがとう (a ri g a to u) means "thank you". [(Re]member when we learned to bow?) ぼくはだいすけです [(bo]ku wa da i su ke de su) means "I'm Daisuke".

だいすけ
DA I SU KE
Here's my name in hiragana. (The first letter is "ta" but we add those two little marks to change "ta" to "da")

さようなら
SA YO U NA RA

Guess what this means!

KATAKANA

[Ther]e are also 50 other letters called katakana. They [make] the same sounds as hiragana, but they look a [little] more angular and pointy. These days they're mainly [used] to write foreign words and names

ダイスケ
DA I SU KE
Here's my name in Katakana. It's completely different from hiragana!

アメリカ
カナダ

What's this country?

How about this one?

メリカ
ME RI KA

ナダ
NA DA

Good job! I hope you enjoyed learning to write Japanese!

Shinto, found only in Japan, is based on nature, purification and blessing. The oldest shrines date back thousands of years.

Wash your hands and rinse your mouth before entering.

The altar has a n in the center, and leaves, rice, and are offered

Ring a bell, bow, and clap your hands at the altar.

Torii gates (center) are usually plain, but may be beautifully decorated, like this one in Kyoto.

Children dressed for "7-5-3" festival

Charms for prote and wooden plaqu for individual pray are sold. You can get your fortune. people tie their fo papers to nearby

November 13

Today was a fantastic, sunny day, and Mrs. M. suggested a visit to a shrine. She said it's a prayer place for Shinto, the religion of Japan. It turned out to be really cool. The shrine was like a big park. First we passed under a huge gate and stopped at a little covered fountain to wash our hands. Then we walked along a gravel path to a big old wooden building which was open at the front. We weren't allowed to take pictures, but inside I could see a kind of table with bottles and leaves in vases and a round mirror at the top. There was a long box in front of us with slats in the top, and Mr. M. gave us each a coin to drop in. We shook a big rope to ring a bell and clapped our hands — he said it was to get the gods' attention before praying. After that we went to a little shop and bought charms — Daisuke and I bought ones for studying and Mr. M. bought one for traffic safety. I asked Mrs. M. about Shinto gods and she said a lot of them are like nature spirits, who live in trees, rocks, mountains, the sun, and other things like that. On our way out, some little kids came in all dressed up in beautiful kimono. Mr. M. said this is the "7-5-3" festival, when parents bring their kids to pray that they'll grow up safe and healthy. When we got home, we looked in the photo album at Daisuke's and Mari's 7-5-3 festival photos. I told Daisuke he looked really cute, and he hit me on the arm.

Ropes are often tied round rocks and trees sacred to Shinto.

Just for Kids!

Well, I've been here almost 3 months already. I thought I'd wri down some of the things I've bee doing with Daisuke and Mari in ou free time. It turns out Japanes kids love a lot of the same thing do — snacking, watching TV, rea comics, playing electronic games But the KINDS of things are completely different!

Japanese supermarkets are FULL of snacks! Daisuke's favorite is "Toppo". It's a kind of long cookie stick filled with chocolate. Mari likes "Apollo", a little cone-shaped chocolate with strawberry flavor. Both these snacks have been around for years. Apollo came out at the time of the Apollo moon-walking space mission! That was like 1970! I like both of these, and I've also discovered a rice cracker with peanuts that is really yummy!

The Muratas have a game system on their TV, and both Daisuke and Mari like to play virtual ping pong. They also have games, but Mrs. M. only allows a half hour of games on school

Hard!

Harder!

HARDEST!

Sometimes Daisuke and Mari play traditional games. Daisuke likes "kendama". It's a hand-held wooden toy with a ball attached by a string. You have to get the ball onto the cups or impale it on the central prong. It's really hard! Mari plays "otedama", a girls' juggling game using little cloth bags filled with dry beans.

Throw!   Pick up!   Catch!

Manga are Japan's version of comic books, some are written mostly for boys, but girls have their share too. I already talked about Daisuke's manga — gory samurai or historical ones. Mari's manga are fairy tales, older literature, or romantic ones. Daisuke said some manga are available in English, so I'm going to have a look in the bookstore. By the way, we're going to take a trip to Osaka next week all by ourselves! I can't wait!

its. Of course
watch regular
V too. Daisuke
es this show
where athletes
complete a really
weird obstacle
course against
the clock!

TRAIN TRIP

To: momndad@yippee.com

Hi you guys! Check out the attached photos of our trip to Osaka on December 10. It took an hour to get there from Daisuke's house. Osaka is a huge commercial and cultural center, second only to Tokyo. So many restaurants! The saying in Japan is, "Eat till you drop in Osaka!"

Here we are getting off the train in the brand-new Osaka Station. The yellow stripe on the ground has raised dots to help blind people walking. Those stripes are everywhere!

We took a river boat ride and saw C
Castle from the boat. Osaka has tor
rivers. Daisuke said there are more
800 bridges in the city!

In the arcade were lots of awesome games. We tried a drumming game. It was really hard! Daisuke beat me by a mile.

We got on the subway too. I heard Japan had a lot of trains, but wow! glad Daisuke knew where we were going, anyway.

Here's where we ate lunch. This restaurant serves tako-yaki, which are roasted dumplings with octopus meat inside. (It's a lot tastier than it sounds!)

After walking around for a while we went to a very classy cake shop. Look at those cakes shaped like chessboards! They were really pricey. We just ordered juice.

We headed home about 4:00. Mari totally crashed in the train! A lot of other people were sleeping on the train too. It's like a national hobby!

December 28

This must be the busiest week of my whole stay in Japan. We had a small Christmas party on the 24th, with a little tree on top of the TV, Kentucky Fried chicken for dinner, a cream cake with strawberries (??) and presents for the kids. (Mr. and Mrs. M. gave me a really nice calendar.) Right after Christmas we swung straight into cleaning the whole house

Christmas

Christmas in Japan is mainly for children, and an important "date" for young people and their sweethearts. There are light shows on Christmas Eve, but on the 25th, it's business as usual.

VS

DECORATION

At the front door, people put a "kadomatsu" with the 3 lucky plants: pine, bamboo, and plum.

The "kagami-mochi" is in the main room. Large rice cakes symbolize abundance and health. A mandarin orange is on top.

(I'm the window washer), shopping, decorating, and making special food, all before New Year, which is MUCH bigger than Christmas. I feel like everything is turned upside down! It's weird to think we have things, like Christmas, that are really important to us, and at the same time, people in other parts of the world are making a big deal out of completely different things, like New Year.

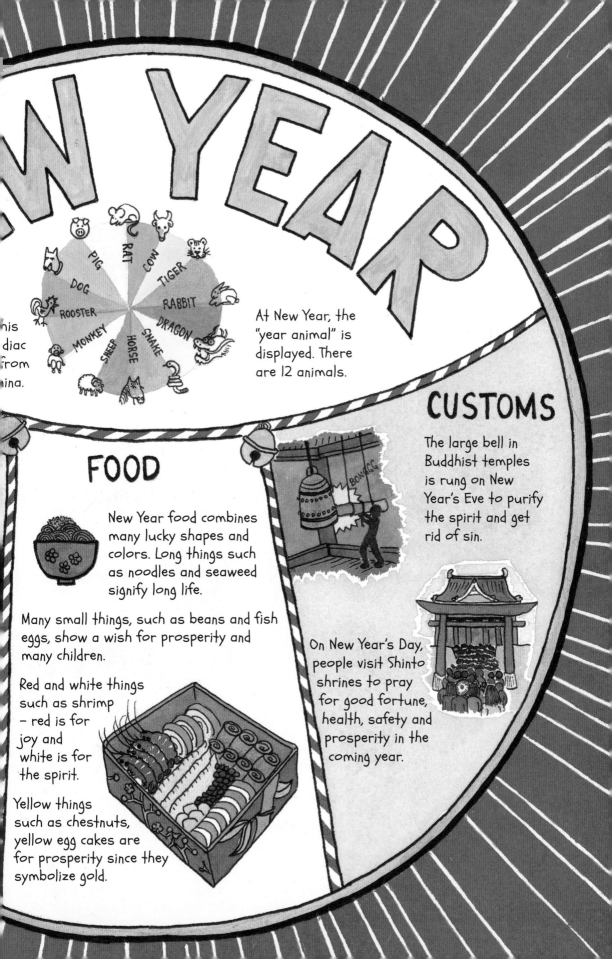

PIG RAT COW TIGER RABBIT DRAGON SNAKE HORSE SHEEP MONKEY ROOSTER DOG

his
diac
rom
ina.

At New Year, the "year animal" is displayed. There are 12 animals.

CUSTOMS

The large bell in Buddhist temples is rung on New Year's Eve to purify the spirit and get rid of sin.

BONNGG

FOOD

New Year food combines many lucky shapes and colors. Long things such as noodles and seaweed signify long life.

Many small things, such as beans and fish eggs, show a wish for prosperity and many children.

Red and white things such as shrimp – red is for joy and white is for the spirit.

Yellow things such as chestnuts, yellow egg cakes are for prosperity since they symbolize gold.

On New Year's Day, people visit Shinto shrines to pray for good fortune, health, safety and prosperity in the coming year.

KARUTA

Happy Holidays! We play a lot of games at New Year, and my favorite is karuta, a matching game played with special cards. I think I'm pretty good at it!

TYPES OF KARUTA
"One Hundred Poets" (Hyakunin-isshu) for older kids and adults

This game is based on poems written about 1000 years ago – but it's not boring at all, it's really cool. There are 2 sets of cards. Players try to beat each other to the cards with the last half of the poem written on them, as the reader reads out the first half. You pretty much have to know all 100 poems really well in order to win. We study this game in school and there are always tournaments around New Year.

"100 Poets" matches are played on TV at New Year. The players wear beautiful kimono.

MAKE OWN

You need 52 pieces of card stock or cardboard (not paper, the cards have to be strong!). A good size is about 4 inches square.

For an extra challenge make a double deck! You need 104 cards for this! Use capital letters with place names (like Alabama, Boston, China, etc.) and small letters for things (airplane, book, cat, etc.).

Traditional Japanese card-matching game! Let's learn to play and make our own set!

Hiragana cards (Iroha karuta) for school-age kids In this version, the 2 sets are based on the hiragana alphabet (remember Daisuke's writing challenge?). One set has a hiragana and a picture, and the other one has a clue. Players search for the picture cards as the reader reads out the clue cards.

HOW to PLAY!

★ You need someone to read the clue cards (my mom usually reads for us) and 2 or 3 players.

★ Sit in a circle on the floor. Spread the picture cards out in the middle.

★ When the reader reads out the clue, try to spot the correct card before anyone else does. When you find the card, grab it!

★ Keep going until all the cards have been picked up. It gets pretty exciting toward the end when there are only a few cards left!

★ Count the cards you got. If you collected the most cards, YOU WIN!

Last time I beat the pants off Dan and Daisuke!

OUR ET!

u can make your own set of ruta based on ABCs. It's easy!

★ For each letter, make 2 cards. Write a word or sentence on the clue card, and the corresponding ABC and a picture on the picture card. Color or decorate them however you like.

But why stop at ABCs? Anything that matches can be a karuta game – like famous sports figures with their sports, countries with their flags, or whatever! You just ed enough cards to make it fun – about 30 or 40 pairs more. Go nuts! Have Fun!

have fun!

MAKING MOCHI

December 28

It was snowing this morning! We were all up really early because we had to make mochi. This is special rice that is pounded into a soft dough and shaped into New Year decorations. I heard that not many people still make mochi the old-fashioned way like the Muratas. We didn't have breakfast because we'd be eating the fresh mochi.

Japanese love mochi any time, roasted and eaten with nori and soy sauce.

First, Mr. and Mrs. M. set up the wooden box steamers on top of a kettle boiling on a gas ring. This was in the breezeway next to the kitchen. It was pretty cold out there. While the rice was steaming in the boxes, we prepared other boxes to hold the mochi and toppings to eat it with.

There was grated daikon, sweet soy sauce, and sweet soybean powder that tasted a bit like peanut butter. My job was grating the daikon. It took me ages!

...lly the rice was done. Mr. M. ...ed it in a huge wooden mortar ...e of a whole tree trunk. Then ...tarted mushing up the rice with ...ng-handled wooden mallet. Mrs. ...ut some salt into the rice then ...d close by. She dipped her hand ...old water and turned the ...aming hot rice really fast. Then ... pounding began! Daisuke took a ...n with the mallet, but Mr. M. says ...needs to grow up some more!

RHYTHM OF MOCHI

① The man raises the mallet and the woman quickly turns the mochi.

...e man ...ounds ...e mochi ...d the ...oman wets ...er hand in cold water.

We pounded 2 more batches of mochi -- small round flat ones, bite-size ones for soup, and loaf-shaped ones that you can slice like bread and roast up. Shaping all these was Mari's job. The last time, they let me pound a few times. The mallet is SUPER heavy and hard to manage. Afterward we took all the things outside and washed them. That was cold! We went back inside and warmed up with hot coffee. (I had toast too.) I think making AND eating mochi would take some getting used to!

When the mochi was smooth, Mrs. M. made two big round pieces for the main decora-tion. Then she divided the rest into the topping bowls. ...he Muratas ate a lot. I had ...ne, but I have to say that, ...K, it was really stretchy ...nd gluggy. I like regular ...rice better!

January 4

I can't believe it's already time for me to go back home. Tomorrow the Muratas are going to take me to the airport. Mr. M. said I'll get back the day I lost when I came, so I'll arrive back home almost the exact same time I leave Japan! Now I'm packing up my suit-case and looking at all the great souvenirs I collected, and remembering all the fun I had. I feel happy. And I feel sad. Weird.

Here's one the origa flowers I r for Respe Aged Day. seems li years ago

This pack of nori is from my first breakfast here. Hope I can get more in the States!

BEAUTIFUL Japan

Souv

This is the calendar Mr. and Mrs. M. gave me for Christmas. It'll look great in my room!

At the shodo class Daisuke wrote my name (Dan) for me 3 different ways.

Daisuke, Mari and I all got the same keychain at the octopus restaurant when we went to Osaka.

Here's the charm I got at the Shinto shrine to protect me against danger.

On the plane going home now. I sure did a lot of things in Japan, but there were also a lot of things I didn't get to do, either because it was the wrong season or because I was just too busy! Anyway I made a list of things I don't want to miss NEXT time I come to Japan...

* After playing that game in Osaka, I really want to see the traditional drumming! I saw just a bit of this on TV - it's so exciting! Daisuke says it's even better in the flesh!

* Next time I want to visit in Spring! I'll be able to see the cherry blossoms! Also, Girls' Day and Boys' Day are both in spring. On Boys' Day they put up huge fish banners called carp streamers. In the photo I saw, they look like they're swimming through the sky.

* I asked Mr. M. what would be at the top of his "must-see" list of historic buildings. He said, the Great Buddha at Nara, and he showed me a photo. It's so big that Daisuke, Mari and I could easily sit together on the palm of its hand (not that we'd be allowed to). Nara apparently also has a big park with tame deer wandering around loose. I'd like to see that.

* If I visit in summer, I'll be able to see the annual high school baseball tournament. This is really huge. The finals are played in August on national television, but Daisuke says it's better to go to the actual stadium, which is near Osaka. They have cheerleading squads, brass bands, and everything! That sounds amazing!

* I think it would be fun to see some traditional theater. Bunraku especially sounds fascinating - it is performed with large puppets, and all the words are spoken by a special singer. In summer there is children's Bunraku, a program with lots of comedy and ghost stories!

Other things on my list: Japanese paper art - kites, fans, and lanterns! Swords and armor!

See you Japan! I AM COMING BACK!